BEAR HUNTING

by Tyler Omoth

FOCUS READERS

WWW.FOCUSREADERS.COM

Focus Readers is distributed by North Star Editions:
sales@northstareditions.com | 888-417-0195

Produced for Focus Readers by Red Line Editorial.

Photographs ©: Gfed/iStockphoto, cover, 1; Predrag Vuckovic/iStockphoto, 4–5; A. G. Wallihan/Library of Congress, 7; andipantz/iStockphoto, 8–9; Rich Legg/iStockphoto, 11; Ben Schonewille/iStockphoto, 13; Sam Cook/MCT/Newscom, 14 (top left); Nataliamarc/iStockphoto, 14 (top right); mkaminski/iStockphoto, 14 (bottom left); Allocricetulus/Shutterstock Images, 14 (bottom right); isifoto/iStockphoto, 15 (top left); Tina Fields/iStockphoto, 15 (top right); avant-g/iStockphoto, 15 (bottom left); beachnet/iStockphoto, 15 (bottom right); Lynn Bystrom/iStockphoto, 16–17; Manamana/Shutterstock Images, 19; splendens/iStockphoto, 21; Anagramm/iStockphoto, 22–23; LuCaAr/iStockphoto, 25; Sandra San/Shutterstock Images, 26–27; Barashenkov Anton/iStockphoto, 29

ISBN
978-1-63517-224-9 (hardcover)
978-1-63517-289-8 (paperback)
978-1-63517-419-9 (ebook pdf)
978-1-63517-354-3 (hosted ebook)

Library of Congress Control Number: 2017935874

Printed in the United States of America
Mankato, MN
June, 2017

ABOUT THE AUTHOR

Tyler Omoth is the author of more than two dozen books for children on topics ranging from baseball to Stonehenge to turkey hunting. He loves going to sporting events and taking in the sun at the beach. Omoth lives in sunny Brandon, Florida, with his wife.

TABLE OF CONTENTS

CHAPTER 1

POWERFUL PREDATORS

You're deep in the woods on a rugged hillside. A large black bear is moving across the open meadow below. You move toward the bear, taking care to stay downwind. You raise your rifle and aim just behind the bear's shoulder. Then you squeeze the trigger. It's a hit!

Forests are good places to find bears.

Humans have hunted bears since prehistoric times. They ate the bear meat. They also used the bear's heavy **pelt** to make warm clothing. Early hunters used spears and traps to take down these huge animals.

In medieval Europe, people began using dogs to hunt bears. Weapons such as guns and bows allowed hunters to

BEAR MEAT

Many hunters enjoy eating bear meat. The meat can vary in flavor depending on what the bear had been eating. Meat from a bear that ate mostly berries will taste different than meat from a bear that ate mostly fish. All bear meat should be cooked thoroughly.

Hunters in the late 1800s set traps to catch bears.

shoot farther, too. Hunters no longer needed to get as close to bears. This helped make bear hunting much safer.

Most hunters today do not need the bear's meat or pelt for survival. But the thrill of hunting bears is still very much alive.

CHAPTER 2

HUNTING METHODS

There are two main methods of bear hunting. They are called stalking and baiting. Hunters who stalk bears travel on foot. They watch for signs that bears are nearby. Common signs include scratch marks on trees, piles of **scat**, and prints in the mud or snow. Bears are often found in places with plenty of trees and shrubs.

Bears scratch tree bark to mark their territory.

But they can also live in mountains and swamps. After hunters spot a bear, they **trail** the bear until there is a good opportunity for a shot.

Hunters who bait bears usually sit in a **tree stand**. They put out bait. The bait smells like something a bear would eat. Popular baits use the smell of black licorice and popcorn. Bears are attracted to these smells. They come closer to the hunter. As a result, it is easier for the hunter to get a good shot.

When hunters think they see a bear, they use their binoculars to get a better look. By confirming that it is a bear, the hunters reduce the risk of hurting

Hunters often practice their aim at shooting ranges before the hunting season begins.

someone or shooting the wrong kind of animal. Hunters may also use rifle scopes to confirm targets. They may use laser range finders as well. The hunter aims the range finder at a bear or another target.

The range finder measures the distance between the hunter and the target.

Bear hunters also choose between two kinds of weapons. Many use guns. Hunters who plan to shoot bears from a long distance often use high-powered rifles. Hunters who expect to get closer to bears tend to use shotguns instead. Shotguns do not have long ranges, but they are powerful. Hunters who bait bears often use shotguns.

Other hunters prefer the challenge of hunting with bows and arrows. There are many kinds of bows, including traditional bows and **compound bows**. A compound bow's **pulleys** make it easier

Compound bows use pulleys to increase a shot's power.

for the hunter to **draw** the string back. Each hunter should choose a bow that is powerful enough for the hunt but easy enough to draw and shoot.

A successful bear hunt with a bow and arrow requires a well-placed shot. It takes a lot of practice to learn how to aim.

BEAR HUNTING SUPPLIES

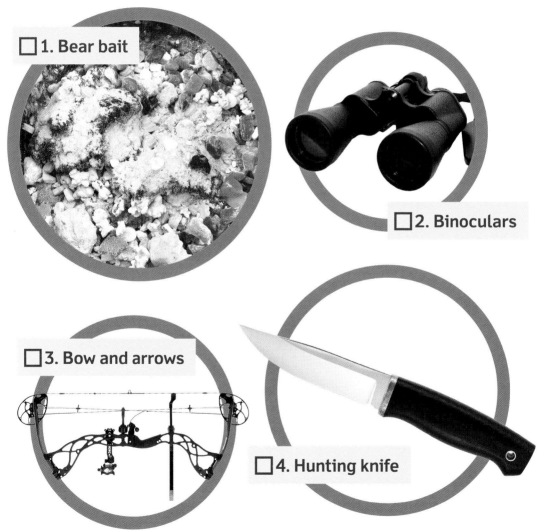

☐ 1. Bear bait

☐ 2. Binoculars

☐ 3. Bow and arrows

☐ 4. Hunting knife

☐ 5. Rifle

☐ 6. Rifle cartridges

☐ 7. Rifle cleaning kit

☐ 8. Tree stand

CHAPTER 3

KNOW YOUR SPECIES

Hunters in North America pursue three main types of bears. Each kind presents a different set of challenges.

American black bears are the smallest bear species in North America. They range from 200 to 600 pounds (91 to 272 kg). Because of their size, they are the most popular bear for bowhunting.

American black bears live in Canada, the United States, and Mexico.

Their varied diet also makes them prime targets for baiting. Black bears roam freely. They cover many miles each day. This can make them hard to track.

The grizzly bear is a member of the brown bear family. Grizzlies live in the western United States and Canada. A

POLAR BEARS

Polar bears are the largest species of bear in North America. But most hunters do not pursue them. For many years, only the Inuit people were allowed to hunt polar bears. Today, a few tags are released each season to non-Inuit hunters. These hunters are still required to have an Inuit guide. This guide receives any meat from a successful bear hunt.

Grizzlies eat fruit, nuts, and fish.

stream with salmon is a good spot to find grizzlies. They may also fish near rivers and lakes. These large bears can weigh more than 800 pounds (363 kg). They can become very aggressive when threatened.

They sometimes attack instead of running away.

Kodiak bears are the third major type of bear hunted in North America. Kodiak bears are another type of brown bear. They are found only in the Kodiak islands in Alaska. Kodiak bears can be up to 10 feet (3.0 m) tall when standing on their hind legs. Adult males often weigh 1,000 pounds (454 kg).

Hunting Kodiak bears can be very dangerous. A hunter must stop the bear with just one shot. The animal's huge size makes this challenging. Hunting Kodiak bears with a bow and arrow is especially difficult.

Bear hunters often hunt in groups for safety.

Hunters must be cautious when approaching any kind of bear. Bears have fairly good eyesight. But they use their powerful senses of hearing and smell to detect food and danger. A bear is likely to hear or smell a hunter before the hunter can see the bear. Hunters should make sure to stay downwind from a bear.

CHAPTER 4

SAFETY TIPS

Bear hunters must know how to handle their guns or bows safely. A hunter should always treat a gun as if it is loaded. The gun's safety should be left on until the hunter is ready to fire. Hunters who use bows should keep their arrows in a quiver with a closable top until they are ready to shoot.

It is important to be careful when loading a rifle.

Hunting group members should create a plan so that each person knows where the others are at all times. Hunters should be positioned so they cannot accidentally shoot one another.

When tracking a bear, hunters must pay close attention and not get too close. Bears can attack when aggravated. Wounded bears can be dangerous, too. If a bear attacks, hunters should not run. Instead, they should wave their arms, make noise, or aim for the bear's eyes.

Sows with cubs are especially dangerous. Hunters should never get between a sow and her cubs. The sow may see this as a threat. A hunter who

A mother bear can be very protective of her cubs.

does get between a sow and her cubs should not fight back. Instead, the hunter should play dead. The sow may stop attacking if she believes the threat is gone.

CHAPTER 5

NATURE-FRIENDLY HUNTING

Governments create hunting seasons to help bears survive. Each state or province has its own hunting seasons. These seasons vary based on the type of bear. Hunters should be sure to know the rules for their area. They must also buy hunting licenses. A license tells the hunter what kind of bear is legal to hunt.

Grizzly bears can often be found fishing for salmon in streams.

It also tells the hunter what size the bear must be. Shooting the wrong type of bear will hurt the area's bear population. But following the guidelines helps keep the bear population stable. Money from license sales also helps fund programs that **preserve** the bears' natural **habitats**.

Hunters can help protect the bears' habitats. They should not leave anything behind at the hunting site. For example, they should pick up used rifle shells and shotgun slugs. Hunters should dispose of the shells or slugs properly after they leave the hunting site. Otherwise, the shells and slugs could hurt the animals that live in the area.

When tracking a bear, a hunter often looks for footprints.

Hunters should also track down any bears they shoot. Tracking a wounded bear can be difficult and dangerous. But hunters should not let a wounded animal suffer. By being careful and following guidelines, hunters can help make sure that others will be able to enjoy hunting in the future.

FOCUS ON
BEAR HUNTING

Write your answers on a separate piece of paper.

1. Write a letter to a friend explaining the main ideas of Chapter 2.

2. Would you rather hunt bears by baiting or stalking? Why?

3. Which type of bear is found only on islands in Alaska?
    - **A.** grizzly bear
    - **B.** Kodiak bear
    - **C.** black bear

4. Why should a hunter try to stay downwind from a bear?
    - **A.** so that the hunter can smell the bear
    - **B.** so that leaves from nearby bushes will not get in the way
    - **C.** so that the wind does not carry the hunter's scent to the bear

Answer key on page 32.

GLOSSARY

compound bows
Bows that use a series of pulleys.

draw
To pull back the string on a bow.

habitats
The type of places where plants or animals normally grow or live.

pelt
An animal's skin and fur.

preserve
To protect something so that it does not change.

pulleys
Wheels with grooves that a rope or chain runs through.

scat
The waste of an animal.

sows
Female bears.

trail
To follow a scent or track in order to catch an animal.

tree stand
A platform that is perched up in a tree.

TO LEARN MORE

BOOKS

Carpenter, Tom. *Big Game Hunting: Bear, Deer, Elk, Sheep, and More*. Minneapolis: Lerner Publications, 2013.

Chandler, Matt. *Bear Hunting for Kids*. North Mankato, MN: Capstone Press, 2013.

Law, Andrew. *We're Going Big-Game Hunting*. New York: PowerKids Press, 2017.

NOTE TO EDUCATORS

Visit **www.focusreaders.com** to find lesson plans, activities, links, and other resources related to this title.

INDEX

Answer Key: 1. Answers will vary; **2.** Answers will vary; **3.** B; **4.** C